Bib
Headship
and the
Ordination
of
Women

by

Colin Craston

Team Rector of St. Paul with Emmanuel, Bolton
Vice-Chairman of the Anglican Consultative Council

GROVE BOOKS LIMITED
Bramcote Nottingham NG9 3DS

CONTENTS

THE COVER PICTURE

is by Peter Ashton

FOREWORD TO SECOND EDITION

It is now two years since the first edition of this Booklet was published, and, as this second edition goes out, the time of the Lambeth Conference of 1988 is drawing near. Thus the issues in the debate about the ordination of women to the priesthood and the episcopate have sharpened. For many Anglicans the main question now concerns the authority of any one part of the one catholic Church to act independently of other parts in adapting the historic pattern of the ordained ministry by including women in each order. Headship, primary leadership in mixed communities of men and women, remains, however, a crucial issue for others. As a continuing contribution to that aspect this Booklet, unchanged apart from tiny correction of printing errors, is re-issued in time for the Lambeth Conference but with the forthcoming Church of England debate in dioceses, deaneries, and parishes, also in mind.

Colin Craston
6 May 1988

First Edition June 1986
Second Edtition May 1988

ISSN 0144 - 171X

ISBN 1 85174 082 1

INTRODUCTION

> 'We must develop opportunities for the ministry of women in the church – as long as we don't appoint them Vicars or Bishops! That would be to breach the principle of "headship" set forth in scripture.'

So runs the thinking of many opposed to the ordination of women to the second and third orders of ministry, the priesthood and the episcopate. They are committed to the authority of scripture, they do not wish to contravene its plain teaching. Arguments against the ordination of women from Catholic order and from tradition may weigh less with them. They accept that the order of the church may be modified in response to the Spirit's leading as times change. They may not be impressed by the argument that a woman's sexuality debars her from receiving the grace of orders – in other words, that 'it would not take' if a woman went through an ordination service – because they do not regard ordination or grace in those terms. And the idea that only a male can represent Christ 'at the altar' carries little conviction with them, for the Christ with whom we are in touch is the ascended Christ and he bears glorified humanity, the whole not just the male half, in his person now; thus the whole church, men and women, represents him on earth, and of the whole a man or woman can be a representative person. Such people may give greater weight to objections touching reunion of the Churches. Ordination of women would raise the barrier between ourselves and Rome and Orthodoxy, if we proceeded to change the inherited tradition without a General Council of the Church – 'but how long would we have to wait for that?' they might ask. And, in any case, there is union with the other great Churches of the Reformation which already ordain women to bear in mind. So, it is this biblical principle of headship, which apparently commits the church for ever to male leadership, which is the real sticking-point for many, mainly but not exclusively in the evangelical tradition. But have they got it right? Has scripture to be interpreted today in that way?

Turning to Scripture

Interpretation of scripture is a never-ending task for the church. Each generation must enquire what the word of the Lord through scripture is for its own day, for each comes to scripture from within a context unique to itself. No other previous times have been like our own. True, there are constants in human history, those eternal truths, those human needs, that remain. But the developments of human history in knowledge, in experience, in opportunities, as well as the pressures, problems and dangers, continually reshape the scenario of life. And Christians have constantly to listen to the voice of their Lord as it first came in a quite different scenario centuries ago. The questions to ask are: What did the message mean to those who first heard it? How was its content, and the way it was applied, shaped by the context in which it was heard? What remains constant for us in our context, and how are we to apply it?

1. MALE LEADERSHIP?

One way of interpreting what we find about headship in the Bible is an insistence on male leadership in the church, not only in our generation but for all time, because it is seen as part of the creation order. So, women may share in the church's ministry, but never individually be leaders over a mixed community at parish or diocesan level. This position is based on the use of certain texts in the Pauline epistles and in the way Paul uses the early Genesis passages. Those texts will require closer examination in due course, but let us recognize now some serious problems this way of interpreting scripture encounters, problems that must at least raise a question over its credibility.

1. The evidence of scripture itself

Whatever may be said about the creation order there are breaches of the principle of male leadership which are claimed to bear God's stamp of approval. Deborah was raised up by God to rule his people. A married woman, yet the one to whom all Israel came for judgment (Judges 4.5), she summoned Barak and gave him orders from God, the carrying out of which led to God's victory (4.23). Barak would not set out without the moral support of her presence (4.8, 9). She was clearly a great leader in a male-dominated society, the saviour of the nation (5.7). Though not so prominent as Deborah, the prophetess Huldah in 2 Kings 22 gives instructions as God's mouthpiece to the king, to the high priest, and to court officials. She has a position of moral leadership even if not exercising the titular headship of a Deborah. Women like Phoebe, Priscilla and Lydia in the New Testament clearly had leadership qualities and in the fluid state of church order in those early days may reasonably be regarded as exercising leadership in local situations. Even some opponents of women's ordination have acknowledged the possibility that they were leaders of house churches, the first kind of Christian assemblies in many places.[1] If Lydia, for instance, the first convert (as far as we know) on European soil, is leader of her household which is baptized when she herself responds to the gospel (Acts 16.14, 15), would she not naturally lead the church in her house?

But, some will reply, Jesus only appointed men as apostles. Does that not commit the church to male leadership for all time? It depends on what we think Jesus was doing. Was he structuring a church, firm and fixed in order for the ages to come? It is more probable that following his vocation as Messiah to re-form Israel as the people of God for service to the nations he was appointing twelve apostles as a re-formed patriarchal band of brothers to be the foundation of the messianic community. How that community should develop in its order and ministry after his death and resurrection he left to the guidance of his Spirit. And what undreamt-of developments and flexibility Pentecost unleashed! – a multiplicity of ministries, prophets (some of them women), evangelists, pastors, teachers deacons (some women), elders, overseers, and extra apostles. The prophecy of Joel used by Peter to account for the new thing at Pentecost joins men and women together in the new ministry – 'Your sons and

[1] G. G. Blum in 'The Office of Women in the New Testament' in *Churchman*, (Vol. 85: 3, 1971) pp.177-78.

daughters will proclaim my message . . . Yes, even on my servants, both men and women, I will pour out my Spirit . . . and they will proclaim my message' (Acts 2.17, 18).

In these consequences of Pentecost we must surely recognize a factor of greatest significance in interpreting New Testament guidelines on ministry, a factor that needs to be set alongside Jesus' choice of men only for the original apostolic band (apparently expanded after Pentecost to include others). It is that the Spirit has freely bestowed gifts of leadership teaching, preaching, irrespective of gender. The church must beware of denying the expression of those gifts.

2. The Contemporary Scene

Then we have to set the 'never a woman' interpretation of headship in the context of the real world of today. This nation is not the first to have a woman as the leader of government. Women exercise leadership over mixed communities in education, industry, medicine, commerce, civic affairs; and a very strong case can be made for women as foremost among the best monarchs our realm has known. If the headship of man is an invariable principle of the creation order, Christians should do all in their power to remove women from these positions of leadership, since such a principle, by definition, applies to society as well as to the church. But, of course, it is only in respect of leadership in the church that the voice of protest against women is heard. We may not be able to change society, it is said, but we can order the church in accordance with God's will in creation. So, is there to be greater restriction on service, less freedom to exercise gifts and develop ministry, not to mention personal fulfilment, for women in the church than in society around? What is the church? Is it not the sign and foretaste of the kingdom, the first fruits of the new creation, the community where men and women are set free as they never can be in their unregenerate state, where they can realize all their potential as the children of God, where barriers of gender, race and class cease to count? Yet, the interpretation of scripture with which we are dealing imposes greater restrictions – even a no-go area! – on redeemed women than they ever encounter in society at large. And all this is in the name of the God who makes all things new.

Some argue that in society, even today, it is natural for man to exercise a leadership and protective role over women. Especially is that to be seen in the family. Father presides at table when the family is together; and is not the church a Christian family? And in a violent society does not a woman need a man's protection? Some rather muddled thinking surfaces here. Whatever customs individual families may preserve, and however convinced some Christians may be that scripture teaches male headship in the family it is quite unrealistic to argue out from the family to society at large. What about all the unmarried women in society? Under whose headship do they come? And in the complex society of today where men and women operate together at work, in civic affairs, in social groups, a man's role in his own family cannot simply be extended to those external areas of life. If he is a leader over other men and other men's wives, as well as single women, he is so by appointment on merit and ability, one hopes, not by any headship-in-family principle. So, given the right qualities, a woman may also be appointed as leader. Some question whether women are psychologically and emotionally equipped for leadership over mixed groups. If generalizations can be dangerous, here is a clear example. There are women undoubtedly good in leadership. The Church of England has itself been blessed with some in its national structures over the years. For over thirty years the Queen has given leadership over nation and Commonwealth which is the envy of the world. And no one should be under the illusion that all men are psychologically and emotionally fit to be leaders. There are some Church of England parishes that know better, to their cost! As for a woman needing a man's protective role, the truth is that it is from male violence the protection is needed, but this has no relevance to the issue of leadership. The removal of every woman from positions of leadership would not remedy that problem one bit. Within the family a man may, but not necessarily will, be able to protect his women folk, but what of all the widows and single women living alone?

The church is a family, it is argued, and so the pattern in the natural family should apply there too. But neither logic nor scripture justifies the application of all facets of family life to God's family. The head of that family is its Lord. Whatever human expressions of headship the church on earth in its many divisions may find beneficial are secondary to his. The Church of England enjoys the benefit of a godly woman as its Supreme Governor. Its bishops pay homage to her as Supreme Governor in matters spiritual and ecclesiastical as well as temporal.

3. The Church around the World

The experience of the church across the world poses severe questions against the strict men-only principle of leadership. And it is not just the existence of many hundreds of Anglican women priests and the growing acceptance of their ministry and leadership in their congregations on which that experience is based. The expansion of the church over the past 150 years owes an enormous debt to women with gifts of evangelism, teaching and pastoral ability, many of them single women, who have crossed the seas to plant young churches. Having planted them, they have been their leaders in early days. The gifts they used were from God, and it would be folly to suppose he only gave them to women because there were not sufficient men willing to go. The women knew they were called of God and, often in face of man-imposed obstacles, obeyed. The leadership they exercised over the emerging churches bore the marks of God's approval no less than that of their male colleagues.

4. Impact on Women

A further factor questioning the credibility of the headship interpretation under review is its impact on many Christian women. To put it mildly they have suffered most unfairly at the hands of the church. Before anyone protests this is merely an emotional judgment, let them read carefully the reports of the proceedings of the Convocations and the Church Assembly of the Church of England over the greater part of this century so far. Early on they were not allowed to be on Parochial Church Councils, let alone higher representative councils of the church. The pay and conditions of service of deaconesses and women workers were generally acknowledged to be deplorable. Fulsome tributes were paid to their devotion, humility, and sacrifice, yet what was done to improve their lot was little and late. Deaconesses were told they were in holy orders, then some years later that they were not, but in an order *sui generis* (that is, of its own kind). Women performing a public ministry could only do it for other women and children. Any men who turned up inadvertently would be offended, or even unhealthily stimulated – so the speeches claimed and, apparently, they swayed the vote. And any ministry must be in the nave or from the chancel steps! Underlying all the arguments was the belief that woman's primary role was the bearing and nurture of children. Any other role in society or church was secondary to that vocation.

But all this is past history, it may be objected. Our synodical forebears were men of their time. What is the relevance now? The relevance is this: running through all the debates decade after decade is the use of scripture to assert the headship of man over woman. All the marks of Christ-like service may be evident, but the scriptures kept her permanently under male leadership, it was argued, as far as the church was concerned, whatever was happening in society. It was not, however, just a particular interpretation of scripture that ran through all the debates, but also a constant and recurrent fear. If the status of women's ministry were enhanced, they would next want ordination to the priesthood. And against that all the arguments heard today were rehearsed again and again.

It is not clear how many of the women who served the church in the past felt a vocation to the priesthood, perhaps very few. What is not in doubt is that many today do deeply believe they are so called. Yet their vocation is not tested. No-one will question the vocation of those large numbers of women whose service overseas contributed to the expansion of the church world-wide. God called them. Nor will any question the vocation of the many women who have served the church at home as deaconesses and women workers. God called them. Yet when a woman wishes to test a vocation to priesthood in the Church of England, the answer is, apparently, God has not called you. Some will say that it is because it is impossible for a woman to receive the grace of orders or to assume the role of *'alter Christus'*. But if those arguments do not weigh, what is left? Is it only the 'subordinate position' argument? If so, the church needs to be very sure it has got it right, otherwise it will be found to be resisting God by not testing the vocation of such as believe they are called. And that perspective is much more serious than is the simple treating of such women unfairly. The past history of the Church of England in the matter of women's ministry does not inspire confidence.

2. BIBLICAL PRINCIPLES – THE OLD TESTAMENT

The foregoing considerations do not amount to a conclusive case against the particular interpretation of scripture that asserts a principle of an exclusively male leadership in the church, but they may be seen as posing a serious question against it. And mentioning them directs our minds to a matter of primary importance. It concerns the way we understand religious truth and so our understanding of what we find in the Bible. Truth cannot be compartmentalized. All truth, whether about the seen or the unseen, whether sacred or secular, whether revealed or naturally perceived is one; and we must ever seek to integrate it as far as our minds dependent on God's Spirit are able. For all truth is God's truth. We cannot be content to keep different realms of truth in distinct packets in the mind, unrelated and unreconciled.

James Denney, a distinguished evangelical theologian of former days, wrote:

> 'The doctrine of God, in the very nature of the case, is related to everything that enters into our knowledge; all our world depends on him; and hence it follows that a systematic presentation of the doctrine of God involves a general view of the world through God, . . . All that man knows – of God and the world – must be capable of being constructed into one, coherent intellectual whole . . . The world is all of a piece; man's mind is all of a piece; and those easy and tempting solutions of the hardest problems which either arrange the world, or the activities of the mind, in compartments, having no communications with each other, are simply to be rejected.'[1]

Why could we not today take seriously an interpretation of the Creation narratives in Genesis that suggested the earth was the centre of the solar system, or even of the Universe, was older than the sun and came into existence some 4,000 years before Christ – interpretations that once prevailed? It is because we seek congruity between our understanding of scripture and what we have learned from astronomy, geology, and other branches of science. In like manner our understanding of what the scriptures have to say about the relationship of men and women in church and society and about the leadership role must be integrated with other truth open to us. And, to say the least, the 'men-only' leadership principle fits uneasily with the considerations touched on earlier.

What do the Scriptures say?

We turn to the text of the Bible, remembering as we do some necessary words of caution. Interpretation of scripture has been going on as long as the written documents have existed. What former generations have made of its message must be weighed with respect and care. The Holy Spirit has been with the church throughout its history. Yet in our day the interpretative task must be done afresh. As we confront and are confronted by the text, our attitude has to be humble and reverent. We must also recognize that we cannot avoid approaching scripture with minds already

[1] James Denney, *Studies in Theology* (Hodder and Stoughton, 1895) pp.1, 4.

conditioned by our culture, experience, convictions. There is no such thing as a blank-mind approach. The very questions we want answered arise from basic presuppositions – some of them formed by our personal spiritual history. The most subtle danger is to assume that our Christian convictions are in no need of challenge from scripture but will simply be confirmed by it. As much as any previous generation, as much as those who first heard God's word in their own situation, we are children of our culture and conditioned by our experience and personality needs. So, for instance, in trying to discover what God is saying to our generation about headship and authority in the church, some will have been much affected in conviction by the considerable changes in the status of women in modern times, while others will be committed in mind to the inherited pattern of male leadership in family, society and church. Let each know himself or herself as fully as may be.

There is something else to be said about interpreting scripture. It follows on from the recognition of the inevitable place of culture – our own and that of the biblical writers – in hearing a word from God. It concerns the actual communication of the word. There is the divine initiative in addressing man, whatever the mode, be it vision, event and guided reflection on the event, voice or growing conviction. But there is also the human side, the perception. And perception can only be from within the knowledge and understanding of the person concerned. What is revealed by God will expand, burst the boundaries of, current understanding, but it will still be within the capacity of that person at that stage of human history to grasp. The full implications of what is revealed may not be seen till later generations, but what is grasped at the time will be recognisable as the truth and relevant to current understanding. This is simply to affirm that revelation is a progressive, educational process, in which the Spirit of God takes a particular and direct initiative, but which is governed at any time by the human capacity for perception. Whether it is an Abraham in the Old Testament, a Peter, John or Paul in the New Testament, or a Christian in the twentieth century, we all 'see through a glass darkly', we only know 'in part'.

Beginning with Genesis

In interpreting scripture it is no bad thing to start at the beginning. It is particularly appropriate when dealing with something that touches the order of creation. The first reference to man and woman is in Genesis 1.27 (repeated in 5.2). The emphasis is on complementary parity – 'God created man (Adam) in his own image . . . male and female he created them.' Adam is the generic name; the Hebrew for male and female presents us with two different words. The next verse points to a joint authority of man and woman over the rest of the created realm. We move into chapter 2. In verses 18-25 we find companionship and partnership are the dominant notes, and specifically – and this is crucial to interpretation – within the marriage bond, the creation of one flesh. In the context of the book this is all 'before the Fall', so whatever interpretation may be put on Genesis 3, we are presumably hearing in chapters 1 and 2 what God's original purpose for mankind is. There is no emphasis on man as head and woman as subordinate. Woman is out of man but they dwell in unity. True, she is described as a 'helper', but as the same word is used of God himself elsewhere in the Old Testament it would be presumptious to imply subordination.

Let us suppose, however, that the headship of man over woman could be deduced from this chapter; it could only apply within marriage. There would appear to be no justification for extending a man's headship to cover relationships in a complex society over all women – other men's wives or single women.

When we turn to chapter 3 we see the effects of man's fallen condition. Man still bears the divine image, but it is now marred. Sin has spoiled the relationship between man and God and between man and woman. Our specific concern is with the latter. Sexual complementarity and mutual desire remain (3.16), but now there is an element of embarrassment. More significantly, however, a subjection of woman to man is now mentioned for the first time. And concerning it two factors must be noted; it is again within the context of marriage, and secondly it is a consequence of the entrance of sin. Subjection is not presented in Genesis as a fundamental principle of God's pattern for all human life but as a dire result of sin, a result all too evident in all societies and cultures throughout the history of mankind.

Those who have come to know the redeeming and renewing grace of Christ and have begun to share in the New Creation recognize that Genesis 3 is not the last word. They must ask: how has the cross of Christ changed the spoiled relationships? To that question we must later address our minds. The time has come to turn to the New Testament passages that bear on the matter of headship.

3. THE NEW TESTAMENT – ESPECIALLY PAUL

What is Paul saying?

It is no exaggeration to describe the Pauline passages about women and their ministry as confusing, especially if taken at face value from our English versions. In 1 Corinthians 14.34, 35 and 1 Timothy 2.8ff. all public ministry is apparently denied to women. But in chapter 11 of 1 Corinthians Paul acknowledges the right of women to pray and prophesy in the congregation. F. F. Bruce, one of the most eminent of biblical exegetes (and a member of the Christian Brethren to boot), comments, 'In the synagogue service a woman could play no significant part . . . In Christ she received equality of status with man: she might pray or prophesy at meetings of the church, and her veil was a sign of this new authority.'[1] The veil had culturally-conditioned, and thus temporary, significance: the authority has permanent value. Another commentator on 1 Corinthians, C. K. Barrett[2], equally emphasizes a full part for women in church worship from chapter 11. He, too, contrary to the interpretation of verse 10 presented in the Good News Bible, affirms the authority of a woman to minister.

We will need to return to these passages later when addressing the question: Why did Paul, apparently, want to shut up the women? But now we can go directly to the heart of our study, headship, and what Paul had to say on it. The principal passage is 1 Corinthians 11.3-16. Space forbids dealing with anything but the alleged principle of male leadership as an abiding factor in the order of creation and applicable both in society over all mixed communities and in the church.[3]

Difficulties in Interpretation

There are three difficulties encountered in interpreting Paul and 1 Corinthians 11.3-16, which should at least question the simple understanding that women are always to be under the authority of men.

1 The meaning of 'head'

Man is the 'head' of the woman, Paul says. In his culture, in the languages he knew and in the one he was writing, what did he understand by 'head'? Both F. F. Bruce and C. K. Barrett in their commentaries say the word denotes source or origin (a clear reference to Genesis 2), rather than leadership, rule, or management. From our culture and understanding we approach the word 'head' in the Bible with assumptions about command, because we know the brain controls the whole body. And we reflect that understanding when we talk about the head of government, a headmaster, or headquarters.

1 F. F. Bruce *1 and 2 Corinthians* (New Century Bible, 1971) p.106.

2 C. K. Barrett *A Commentary on the First Epistle to the Corinthians* (Adam and Chas. Black, 1968).

3 In other words, there is not space to examine New Testament teaching on the relation of husband and wife within marriage. Some Christians are prepared to allow women leaders in society and church, and thus the ordination of women, but still adhere to a headship of the husband in the family. Whether that be a sound position or not, the claim of this Study is that the family situation cannot be argued outwards to the community at large, secular or Christian. To put it briefly, Genesis 2 cannot be applied to the church. There are studies that examine the New Testament teaching on the man-woman relationship in marriage – one such is mentioned in the reference below – and conclude that in Christ any subordination of wife to husband is no longer appropriate. See: Michael J. Williams, 'The Man/Woman Relationship in the New Testament' in *Churchman* (Vol. 91: 1, 1977).

Hebrew has no word for brain. In Hebrew thought the directing centre of the personality was not located in the head, but in the heart and in the guts, a concept taken up in several places in the Greek of the New Testament writings. So, 'the head is not regarded as the seat of the intellect controlling the body but as the source of life'.[1] Both Hebrew and Greek words for head, while clearly denoting the physical head of man or animal, are closely related to origin or source We talk of the head of a river, meaning where it springs from, and indeed that use of the word is found in Genesis 2.10. So when in that same chapter woman is said to be formed out of man we could expect the Hebrew concept of headship of man in relation to woman primarily to indicate source. To quote *The New Bible Dictionary* again: 'when man is spoken of as the head of the woman, the basic meaning of head as the source of all life and energy is predominant.'[2]

But, it may be asked, do we not speak of Christ being head of the church, meaning he is its Lord? Indeed, according to our modern understanding of headship, Christ is Lord of the church, exercising his authority and rule over it. In the language of the New Testament, however, when that relation of Christ to his church is in mind, the word 'Lord' is used, not head. The way Paul uses the word 'head' is confirmed by his reference to Christ in Colossians 1.18: 'Christ is the head of the body, the church; he is its source [or beginning].' In the Corinthian passage Paul avoids 'Lord' in reference to God, Christ and man. And the fact that Christ is described as 'head of every man' strengthens the 'source or origin' interpretation. If Paul had said 'head of every Christian man', or words to that effect, the idea of lordship might have been easier to sustain. But if it is Christ as the agent of creation, the source of life, that is in the apostle's mind, the reference to every man (who has ever lived) is understandable. Of course, in that sense Christ is the head of every woman too. But Paul has a particular reason for tracing the source of woman to man, following the Genesis 2 story. He wants to show that to have 'a head' is to reflect the glory of that head, because he is dealing with a practical problem in the Corinthian church concerning the covering or uncovering of heads, male and female, in worship.

2 Christ's relationship to the Father

We have already begun to touch the second difficulty in interpreting Paul. What is he saying about Christ's relationship to God? According to chapter 11 verse 3, the man-woman relationship and the doctrine of the Trinity are related in some way. We must avoid the risk of reading back into the New Testament writings, and particularly an early letter such as this, a developed Trinitarian theology. Even more, we must not expect to find doctrine expressed in the Greek philosophical terms of the fourth century as in the Nicene and Athanasian Creeds. That said, does Paul mean his readers to understand a real subordination of Christ to God, such as is to be reflected in woman to man? There are passages in the Epistles where Christ in his incarnate humanity submits to the Father, and these echo many of his

1 *The New Bible Dictionary* (IVF, 1962) p.508.
2 *Ibid.* p.508.

own words in the Gospels. But in his essential nature the Son is God, as the prologue to John's Gospel affirms; he always had the nature of God, as Paul himself says in Philippians 2. As the Athanasian Creed puts it, the persons of the Trinity are 'co-equal' and the Son is 'equal to the Father, as touching his God-head'. Before we conclude an emphasis on subordination in 1 Corinthians 11.3 we need substantial proof. Considering the likely interpretation of 'head' and the implications for a Trinitarian theology, that proof seems to be lacking. The more convincing understanding, according to C. K. Barrett, is that Paul is referring to the Father as the *fons divinitatis* (fount of deity) – 'The Son is what he is in relation to the Father.'[1] As the Nicene Creed says, the Son is 'God of [from] God.' Verse 3 then is emphasizing that woman is of (from) man, and he is in that sense her 'head'.

3 The Genesis texts

A third difficulty presented by the Pauline passages is his way of using the Genesis texts. In 1 Corinthian 11.7 he speaks of man as the image and glory of God and woman simply in terms of her relationship to man. It is noteworthy he does not say woman is the image of man, but why does he ignore Genesis 1.27 where both male and female together are in the image of God? It is thought that Paul is following a Rabbinic interpretation of Genesis 2, but must we? In 1 Corinthians 14.35 – which some have suggested is a later interpolation, but for present purposes may be taken as from Paul – he instructs women, or possibly 'wives', to be in submission (presumably to their husbands, in the light of the next verse) 'as also the law says.' The word for submission does not denote the obedience which, for instance, children owe to parents (Eph. 6.1) but a willing deference which all Christians are to show to one another (Eph. 5.21).

Paul's reference to the law must be an allusion to God's edict after the Fall in Genesis 3.16. But does Paul intend us to take the declaration of the husband's rule over his wife as part of that Law of God which is good, which is for man's true welfare, and which glorifies himself? Or, does not the context with references to pain, sorrow and struggle indicate a statement concerning a dire consequence of sin?

In 1 Timothy 2.14, where again the theme appears to be a denial of all public ministry to women, the Fall is further referred to. This time Genesis 3 is used to put a greater share of the blame on the woman than on the man for the entry of sin. But, granted the first step is taken by Eve, would a reading of Genesis 3 without this Pauline gloss suggest Adam is less culpable? True, he tries to put the blame on her, and in so doing begins a long tradition of masculine attitude towards woman as temptress. Are we, again, confined solely to the Pauline interpretation?

The Use of the Old Testament by New Testament Writers

This Pauline use of the early chapters of Genesis may profitably be considered in the light of the general use of Old Testament texts by New Testament writers. We might have expected meticulous care and exact interpretation of what to them all were the sacred writings. But that is certainly not always so. At times the interpretation of the Old Testament appears to

1 *Op. cit.* p.249.

be exceedingly arbitrary. In Hosea 11.1, referring to Israel's deliverance at the Exodus, the Lord says, 'Out of Egypt I called my son.' Matthew 2.15 says that Jesus' sojourn as a young child in Egypt was a direct fulfilment of the Hosea text. Matthew again in the same chapter (verse 23) regards the residence of Jesus in Nazareth as a fulfilment of the prophecy identifying the Messiah as a Nazarite, whereas it is clear from Judges 13 that the term has nothing to do with that city. Sometimes one Old Testament book is named but another quoted. (Mark 1.2 and Matthew 27.9 are examples). The Matthew 27 example is from a situation in the New Testament where a very strange use of Old Testament texts is made. In Matthew 27.3-9 the death of Judas Iscariot is recorded. And in Acts 1.18-19 it is referred to again in the appointment of his successor. Not only do the two accounts differ – in one Judas hangs himself, in the other he fell to his death, in Matthew the chief priests buy a cemetery with the betrayal money after his death, in the Acts Judas buys the field before his death – but the way both apply Old Testament writings would strike any preacher or commentator today as quite amazing. The Zechariah passage (Matthew names him Jeremiah) is about the prophet being paid wages for minding sheep and then casting them into the Temple treasury (or giving them to a potter). As well as the Zechariah quotation, Matthew may have in mind an incident in Jeremiah (32.7-9) where that prophet purchases a field from a relative as a prophetic sign – hence the attribution of the quotation to Jeremiah. Whatever the explanation it remains surprising that Matthew can see in either passage a direct reference to Judas' action. Similarly in Acts 1 when Peter addresses the need for a successor to Judas he quotes from two Psalms (69.25 and 109.8), neither of which could be said to bear directly on the situation although certain features do correspond.

Paul himself sometimes displays a freedom in adapting or altering Old Testament passages. In 1 Corinthian 14.21 in dealing with speaking in tongues he quotes Isaiah 28.11-12, adapting a reference to foreigners teaching God's people a lesson. In Ephesians 4.7ff. Paul speaks of the ascended Christ distributing his gifts to all members of the church. He illustrates the truth from Psalm 68, where the victorious king returns to Sion in truimph, leading his captives, and then 'receives' gifts (presumably from his conquered peoples). Paul changes it to 'giving' gifts as he quotes the Psalm, doubtless because that is the main point he wants to make. It has been suggested he was using some Jewish interpretation of the verse, but most commentators, including Calvin, regard the alteration as Paul's.

How are we to account for this kind of use of the Old Testament, which if followed by a preacher or commentator today could merit a rebuke? The probable answer is that the New Testament writers are following a method of scriptural exposition used in the Judaism of their day. It is known as *'midrash'*, its general meaning 'commentary'. Earle Ellis, a conservative New Testament scholar, says the essence of the method was 'a contemporization of Scripture in order to apply it to or make it meaningful for the current situation.'[1] Old Testament allusions are introduced to illumine or explain the matter under review. The method may be criticized, as Earle Ellis says, but we should admit that our own modern methods of interpretation are deficient. We may question the interpretations of past ages, but rarely can we achieve total agreement in our understanding of the text.

[1] E. Earle Ellis, 'How the New Testament uses the Old' in *New Testament Interpretation* (ed. I. Howard Marshall) (The Paternoster Press, 1977) p.202.

The Situation Paul Faced

What is the significance of these considerations for our Study? They may throw light on Paul's treatment of selected texts from the early Genesis chapters. One thing is certain, he is not attempting a systematic exposition of Genesis as he writes to Corinth, or to his young friend, Timothy (1 Timothy 2.8ff.). Everything points to the Apostle being faced with a difficult pastoral problem in which feelings, including his own, ran high. To deal with it he brings all the arguments he can to bear, including the midrashic use of the Old Testament. There are solid grounds for believing that at Corinth and elsewhere women, or some of them, were causing substantial problems in the public worship of the church. Women from the background of a pagan culture in which they had been conditioned to regard themselves as inferior beings had now found a new status in Christ. Jewish women too had previously no significant part in synagogue worship. Now women could pray and prophesy in the assembly as 1 Corinthians 11.5ff. makes clear. It would appear that some women were exploiting their new found status and succumbing to excesses of self-expression. A reading of the whole Corinthian letter gives the impression of no clearly marked structures in worship but rather of chaotic meetings. Paul undoubtedly wants to bring in some sense of decency and order (1 Corinthians 14.40). It is precisely in that context that Paul tells women 'to keep silence' (chapter 14.34, 35). As he has already acknowledged their right to pray and prophesy in church, what can he mean? Some think he is trying to stop chattering. More likely, according to C. K. Barrett, he is dealing with heated arguments during scriptural exposition. Verse 35 would support that interpretation in its insistence that wives should consult their husbands at home. The same apparent silencing of women in worship is found in 1 Timothy 2.8ff. But again it seems to be within a context of difficulties in worship. Verse 8 expresses the apostle's preference for men 'to pray', and he adds significantly 'without wrath and disputing' possibly indicating the prevalence of controversy. This time, however, women are simply told to learn 'in quietness'. The word does not mean actual silence, but 'a quiet way of life'. In this letter at 3.11 and 5.13 there is clear evidence of trouble from feminine tongues. Paul goes on to forbid women teaching or domineering (as the word 'to have authority' means) over men. Is the problem he encountered in the Corinthian church still around later? If so, Paul must take a strong line – and he plays safe.

So the cultural situation must be recognized. Paul is a man of his own times. He is used to the midrashic method of interpretation. He is dealing with a practical, pastoral problem shaped by conditions in the first century. In his writing there is a struggle going on between his assumptions as a man of his own times and the new order in Christ which he is for ever exploring with the aid of the Holy Spirit. These considerations must be held in mind as from within our own culture we read these parts of the New Testament. Thus, 'The discerning reader should come to the decision that the things Paul is dealing with here are indifferent, neither good nor bad; and that they are forbidden only because they work against seemliness and edification.'[1] The New Testament contains abiding principles formulated by Jesus and his apostles, essential to the well-being of the church in all ages. It also contains *ad hoc* rulings addressed to particular situations in the first century. Distinction between the two must be made.

1 Calvin on 1 Cor. 14.34-35, quoted by C. K. Barrett, *op. cit.* p.333.

4. HEARING GOD'S WORD TODAY

Is it possible by a faithful attention to the Scriptures to conclude that God is telling us in our day to afford to women a full partnership with men in the leadership of the church, so that they are not only admitted to the ordained ministry but, according to individual gifts, may be appointed the leaders of mixed teams or of dioceses? That is our final question. Before attempting an answer one thing should be clear. It concerns the nature of the leadership in the church, the way of exercising authority. Leadership is not to be a one-person dictatorship. It is to be exercised in a consultative way, and in partnership with others. The Anglican pattern in a diocese is best described as Bishop in Council, and requires consultation with clergy and laity. At parish level it calls for team work with lay leaders as well as any other ordained members. There will be a *primus inter pares,* one with whom the buck stops, for in all human institutions the need for an arbiter in unresolved differences will arise from time to time. Above all, authority has to be seen as the authority of loving service. Christian authority is that of the master who washed his quarelling disciples' feet, is supremely that of a crucified man winning hearts and minds by his dying love. Opponents of women's ordination sometimes argue that it is the dominant role of man that qualifies him for leadership, women's role is more passive. Is this not to follow the ways of the world? Christian leaders have another pattern.

A New Creation, a New Order

Earlier we turned from a brief consideration of Genesis 3 with a question unanswered. If a subordination of woman to man, or more accurately of wife to husband, possibly as her instinctive desire towards and dependence on him are taken advantage of to dominate her, is a result of the Fall and not part of the pattern of life God wills, what difference does the cross of Christ make? All Christians know that Genesis 3 is not the last word on relationships. Indeed within that chapter there is immediate promise of a deliverer.

The incarnation, death and resurrection of Jesus brought in a new order, a new creation of men and women redeemed from sin and its effects. Those who by grace are born anew into the redeemed race enjoy immediately deliverance from some of the effects of sin, from other effects they await deliverance. Full pardon, adoption into God's family, the gift of eternal life are already theirs. Salvation from the presence and lure of sin and perfection of character in holiness will only come with their resurrection. But that is not the whole story. There is the in-between time, the life they live as the redeemed but yet not made perfect. In all areas of life they are to enter into the benefits and to realize the possibilities of the new order in Christ. This is where the effects of the cross on human relationships come in.

The cross puts right what the Fall put wrong. It puts right the relationship of the sinner with his holy God. It makes possible the righting of relationships between man and man, man and woman, man and his environment.

How does the cross make that possible? First by revealing that when man is right with his Maker in Christ barriers between man and man come down. The redeemed person accepts his or her restored relationship to God by faith Feelings may or may not enter in The fact is, God declares that person reconciled as he or she trusts in Christ and his word is accepted. So, faith accepts the truth that in Christ all barriers created by sin are down Then faith consciously invokes the power of the cross, the outpoured sacrificial love, to translate what is true in God's purpose into actual experience. Or, to put it another way, to turn divine truth into reality in human living.

This is what Paul undoubtedly has in mind in Galations 3 28 when he speaks of there being in Christ neither male nor female, Jew nor Gentile, bond nor free. He is not thinking only of equal standing in grace of individual believers before God; the letter is deeply concerned with relations between Jewish and Gentile Christians. And from that social context he moves to relations between the sexes. He is not denying the distinctive natures or the complementary roles of men and women There are still Jews and Gentiles (and many other divisions of mankind) with their characteristics and cultures, and still (in his day and ours) the bound and free. But old barriers built by man's sin are demolished and broken or distorted relationships are, in Christ, repaired It may be noted, in passing, that by and large supporters of the ordination of women do not use the Galations 3.28 reference for a kind of uni-sex approach to ministry, as if Paul was saying there are no differences between men and women. Rather, they would rejoice in the difference, longing to see the complementary partnership between men and women enriching the ordained ministry – but more of this later.

So what the cross has made possible Christians are to seek to make real in experience. It was earlier suggested that the way to do that was faith. But any impression of an easy task must be dispelled. For one thing redeemed men and women are still sinners. As Article IX of the Thirty-Nine Articles of Religion puts it, 'this infection of nature (the natural inclination to sin) doth remain, yea in them that are regenerate.' And then, even though they are children of the new order in Christ, they must live within the cultural restrictions and social order of their day. We can illustrate this from one of the divisions in society mentioned by Paul in Galatians 3.28 – the bond and the free. In Christ there is to be a new relationship between master and slave. In Ephesians and Colossians he teaches about this, and when he is faced with a live example of a run-away miscreant slave, Onesimus, now a believer, returning to his Christian master, Philemon, he urges a restoration of relationship only possible in Christ. But nowhere does Paul, or any other New Testament writer, work for or advocate the abolition of the institution of slavery. That was neither possible, nor probably envisaged, in the social order of his day. The time would come when abolition was possible, but it was far off. Thus in Christ the personal relationship between master and slave is transformed, and the barriers that would deny their mutual recognition as equally God's children are down.

Likewise the inner relationship between man and woman is transformed in Christ. Whatever the Fall has introduced into the relationship can be remedied. What this may mean within the context of marriage is not of immediate consequence for this study, although Paul and Peter, writing as we must recognize within the culture of their day, both show the impact of Christ's redemption on the husband-wife relationship. But whether within marriage or in society at large any male domination of woman based on selfishness or resulting in inhibition of woman's full development and potential is both judged and remedied in the cross. Similarly from the woman's side any bitterness or selfish reaction, however understandable if there is a sense of injustice, is to be brought under the healing power of the cross.

The new order is not, however, just about putting wrongs right. It is also about Christ's liberating power, freeing men and women to realize their full potential as the children of God. And so those who are in Christ must strive in his power for changes in the social order wherever it inhibits that development. The inhibitions are not just from within an individual's sinful nature. They are in the structures of society as well. We are recognizing this in the deprived inner urban areas of our towns and cities. We see it in the apartheid system in South Africa. We recognize it in all oppressive regimes. The new order in Christ presents a vision of human living as God will it. It is not just of individual persons made right with God and with other individuals. That is crucial. But it is also about communities ordered in such a way that men and women can be free to be whole, to develop in a climate of justice and equity. Another way of describing this is to speak of the kingdom of God. In one sense the kingdom is here; the church, being the new race of mankind, is the sign and foretaste of it. In another sense the kingdom is not yet. And Christians living in the 'now, but not yet' situation have to strive for the realization in the world of what God wills. They themselves are in the process of being changed, or should be. They have not yet reached the goal set before them in the Christian vision. So, in themselves, and in so far as they may initiate or assist change in society, they are to work towards the fulfilment of the Christian vision.

In respect of the institution of slavery the time came, many centuries after Paul's day, when it could be abolished formally. The changed inner relationship between bond and free made possible in Christ was in the course of time matched by a changed social order. Those Christians who fought so long and at great personal cost, not just against governments and commercial interests but against reactionary church forces, for the abolition saw their struggles as a demand of God's kingdom. Slaves had to be delivered from a system that thwarted their full development as men and women made in God's image. Why did it not happen earlier? From the human side the answer would be, because developments in history did not permit it earlier. The working out of God's purposes in history is not ours to know, but that his hand was in the deliverance we cannot doubt.

And now – Men and Women in a New Partnership

A fundamental question now facing the church in our day is this – has it become possible for the changed personal relationship between men and women established by the cross to be reflected in the social order, and in the church? If the analogy of slavery is applicable we would expect new developments to arise in history to enable now what was not possible or even envisaged in the first century or many following. And that is just what we have seen over the last hundred years or so. Equal educational opportunities, medical discoveries in family planning, technological inventions to ease greatly the burdens of house work, have all transformed the life of the vast majority of women, at any rate in the developed countries This hitherto unimagined enlargement of opportunity for women to share with men in service in all walks of life has not been easy to cope with by men or women. And undoubtedly fallen nature can distort and abuse that which is good. But Christians cannot dodge the question – are the wider opportunities for women to share in fuller partnership with men in service to humanity *of God,* or are they not? If they are, he must be challenging us to co-operate with him in his developing purposes in history.

Some opponents of women's ordination accuse supporters of succumbing to extreme feminist agitation, of wanting the church to copy the ways of the world. That is a gross misunderstanding. Those who want to see women fully sharing in the ministry and leadership of the church believe that in the modern development of enlarged opportunity for women God has provided the matrix in which a new stage in the realization of the vision of Galatians 3.28 may emerge. Inhibitions and barriers to a fuller development of woman's potential, and thus to a more effective partnership with man, which have prevailed since the dawn of human history, can go. Individual women have from time to time, in biblical history and since, overcome them, but now more and more have their opportunity. This, of course, is already happening in society. What an irony it is, that in the church, or parts of it, the realization of the vision encapsulated in Galatians 3.28 is taking longer! If God is leading us through the modern emancipation of women to a fuller expression of his new order in the structures of society, how tragic it would be for the church, the sign and foretaste of his kingdom, to drag its feet!

All this, it should be emphasized, is for a complementary partnership of men and women, just what they were made for, according to Genesis 1.26-30. Both must bring their respective qualities, natures, insights and gifts to the partnership. Women are not to ape men, nor men to think they are complete without the women. Together, not separately, they reflect the image of God, and together they can enrich the ministry and leadership of the church.

It is argued that, because God is presented in scripture in male terms, revealed as Father, and in his incarnation became a male, the leadership of the church must always be male. This is to ignore the motherly qualities also ascribed to God in Scripture. Indeed, if woman is equally in the image of God, as Genesis 1.27 affirms, all her qualities are to be found in him. We need not adopt non-sexist language, addressing God as both he and she. It is certainly not necessary, so long as we avoid thinking of God in exclusively masculine terms, and recognize the need of men and woman in partnership to represent him. In the Jewish culture of his day it could be said that Jesus had to be male. Teacher, rabbi, fulfilment of the 'Son of Man' imagery, the Lamb to be slain as a sacrifice for sin, prophet, priest, king, all these roles demanded a male. But ascended now to the Father he bears not just male humanity but all humanity in his person. He represents all, he may be represented by all.

In emphasizing the complementary partnership that men and women could offer in the leadership of the church we should avoid too rigid stereotypes. The qualities of men and women are not totally different and unshared. Men may possess qualities often characterized as feminine – gentleness, receptivity, for instance. Were they not seen in Jesus? Women may reveal gifts of initiative, robust imperturbable strength in crisis, balanced judgment under pressure. In other words, women can have qualities for leadership, while some men will never make leaders. Our contention is that, with men and women in the ordained ministry, acknowledged gifts not gender should determine the issues of leadership whether in parish or diocese.